Holiday Wrappings

Quilts to Welcome the Season

LORAINE MANWARING
AND SUSAN NELSEN

Martingale®
& COMPANY

Holiday Wrappings:
Quilts to Welcome the Season

© 2008 by Loraine Manwaring
and Susan Nelsen

That Patchwork Place® is an imprint
of Martingale & Company®.

Martingale & Company
20205 144th Ave. NE
Woodinville, WA 98072-8478 USA
www.martingale-pub.com

Printed in China
13 12 11 10 09 08   8 7 6 5 4 3 2 1

Library of Congress Cataloging-in-Publication Data
Library of Congress Control Number: 2008014036

ISBN: 978-1-56477-862-8

Dedication

*To our grandmother,
Susan Blanche
Lyman Knutson.
You always dazzled us,
but especially at
Christmastime!*

Acknowledgments

*With thanks and love to our families
for their never-ending patience,
support, and encouragement.*

Mission Statement
Dedicated to providing quality products
and service to inspire creativity.

Credits
President & CEO: Tom Wierzbicki
Publisher: Jane Hamada
Editorial Director: Mary V. Green
Managing Editor: Tina Cook
Developmental Editor: Karen Costello Soltys
Technical Editor: Robin Strobel
Copy Editor: Marcy Heffernan
Design Director: Stan Green
Production Manager: Regina Girard
Illustrator: Adrienne Smitke
Cover & Text Designer: Regina Girard
Photographer: Brent Kane

Contents

Introduction

We love the holidays! Though each of us has a collection of quilts we use to celebrate the season, neither of us has enough. It was great fun designing these merry quilts. You'll note that most of them are done in the traditional holiday shades of red and green, but as we designed and quilted, it became apparent that each quilt could be adapted for other celebrations and holidays. For example, "Christmas Basket" on page 14 could be filled with a spring bouquet of varied colors; "Merry Mail" on page 4 could be done in shades of red or pink to display special Valentines and notes of love; and black and orange fabrics would transform "Candy Sticks" on page 24 into a collection of Halloween treats. There really are no limitations to what you can create if you let your imagination take over. Look for additional suggestions for adapting these quilts to other special days as you read the "Wrap It Up!" sections throughout this book. We're sure that you'll find additional ways to use these designs.

Our projects call for basic cutting and piecing techniques that are familiar to most quilters. Our step-by-step instructions give details for any special techniques that we use in these projects. If you would like complete information about rotary cutting, basic piecing, preparing backings, adding borders, and binding, you can find many excellent books for beginners at your favorite quilt store.

Happy holidays all year long!

Loraine and Susan

Merry Mail

Skill Level: Confident Beginner ❄❄

Finished Quilt: 45" x 45"

WRAP IT UP! We all love to receive holiday mail from friends far and near. Celebrate the season with this merry quilt that doubles as a place to stash those special cards and letters. This quilt could easily be adapted to display wedding wishes or valentine love notes. — *Loraine*

MATERIALS

Yardage is based on 42"-wide fabric.

1 yard of dark green print for outer and inner borders

¾ yard of red print for binding and middle border

⅝ yard of white print for middle border and border foundation

½ yard *each* of four coordinating medium green prints for the pieced background

½ yard *each* of eight coordinating prints for envelope B

⅜ yard *each* of six coordinating prints for envelope A

2 yards of white flannel to be used in place of batting for envelopes A and B

3 yards of fabric for backing

50" x 50" piece of batting

7 assorted buttons for embellishing the holiday envelopes

CUTTING

All measurements include ¼"-wide seam allowances.

From *each* of the four coordinating medium green prints, cut:

3 strips, 4" x 42"; then crosscut into 21 squares, 4" x 4" (84 total)

From the white print, cut:

4 strips, 2" x 42"

4 strips, 1¾" x 42"; crosscut into:
    2 strips, 1¾" x 37½"
    2 strips, 1¾" x 35"

From the red print, cut:

4 strips, 2" x 42"

5 strips, 2¾" x 42"

From the dark green print, cut:

4 strips, 2" x 42"; then crosscut into:
    2 strips, 2" x 32"
    2 strips, 2" x 35"

5 strips, 4" x 42"

MAKING THE QUILT CENTER

1. Select nine of the green 4" squares and sew a row as shown. Make a total of nine rows. You will have three unused squares. Press in one direction.

Make 9 rows.

2. Sew the nine rows together as shown to complete the quilt center.

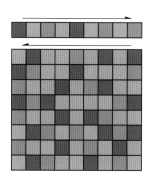

MAKING THE STRIPED MIDDLE BORDER

1. Sew four white and four red 2" strips together, offsetting each strip by 1½" as shown. Press toward the red strips.

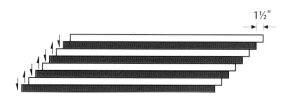

1½"

2. Place the 45°-angle line of your ruler along a seam line and cut twelve 1¾"-wide diagonal segments as shown.

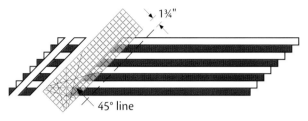

Cut 12 diagonal strips.

3. Sew three segments together to make one long border piece. Repeat with the remaining segments to make a total of four border pieces.

Make 4.

4. Trim two of the border pieces to measure 1¾" x 35" and the other two to measure 1¾" x 37½".

5. Place one of the 35"-long borders on a white 1¾" x 35" strip and machine baste along the center as shown. Repeat with the other 35" border. Basting the pieced borders onto a background strip stabilizes the borders and prevents them from stretching as they are added to the quilt.

6. Baste together the 1¾" x 37½" pieced borders and the 1¾" x 37½" white strips as in step 5.

ADDING THE BORDERS

1. Sew the dark green 2" x 32" strips to the sides of the quilt; then add the 2" x 35" strips to the top and bottom of the quilt. Press toward the borders.

2. Sew the striped 1¾" x 35" borders to the sides of the quilt and the 1¾" x 37½" pieces to the top and bottom. Press toward the borders.

3. Measure the quilt through the vertical center and cut two dark green 4" border strips to this measurement. Sew these pieces to the sides. Measure the quilt through the horizontal center and cut

two dark green 4" border strips to this measurement, joining strips as necessary. Add these borders to the top and bottom of the quilt and press. Remove the basting stitches from the striped border.

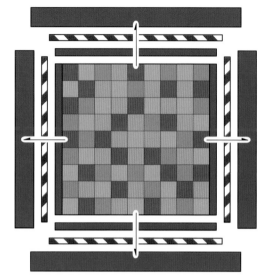

Quilt layout

FINISHING YOUR QUILT AND ADDING THE ENVELOPES

1. Layer the quilt top, batting, and backing; then baste, unless you plan to take your quilt to a long-arm quilter.

2. Hand or machine quilt as desired.

3. Use the red 2¾"-wide strips to bind the edges.

4. Sew a hanging sleeve to the back of the quilt if desired.

PERSONALIZE YOUR QUILT

You may want to add more envelopes to this quilt. Perhaps you would like to leave all of them open so that you have room to store even more cards and letters. Or, if you have no fear of buttonholes, add a buttonhole to each envelope so that you can open and close them as you wish!

Making the Envelopes

1. Enlarge the patterns on pages 8–9 as indicated. From each of the six coordinating fabrics, cut one envelope A. (Three will be linings and three will be outer envelopes.)

2. From *each* of the eight coordinating fabrics, cut one envelope B. (Four will be linings and four will be outer envelopes.)

3. From the white flannel, cut three of envelope A and four of envelope B.

4. Layer one outer piece and one lining piece, right sides together, on a flannel batting piece. Pin together as shown.

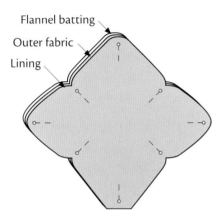

Flannel batting
Outer fabric
Lining

5. Stitch around the edges using a ¼" seam allowance and leaving an opening for turning as indicated on the pattern. Clip the areas indicated, being careful not to cut the stitching.

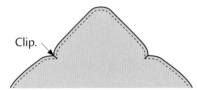

Clip.

6. Turn the envelope right side out and press carefully. Slipstitch the opening closed and then topstitch ¼" from the edge all the way around the envelope.

7. Carefully fold along the dotted lines marked on the pattern and press.

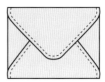

8. Hand sew the bottom flap to the side flaps using a long running stitch. The running stitch will be invisible if you follow the topstitching.

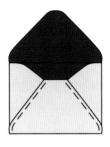

9. Repeat steps 4–8 to make a total of seven envelopes: three using pattern A and four using pattern B.

Attaching the Envelopes

1. Place the envelopes on the quilt center, using the photo on page 4 as a guide.

2. Use a blanket stitch to secure each envelope to the quilt. Sew around three sides of each envelope, by hand or machine, as shown.

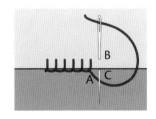

3. Lift each envelope flap and machine stitch across the fold line as shown.

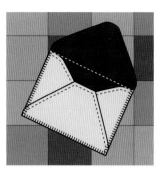

4. Tack the "open" envelope flaps to the quilt so that they will remain open.

5. Tack the "closed" envelope flaps down.

6. Sew the assorted buttons to the envelopes as a final embellishment.

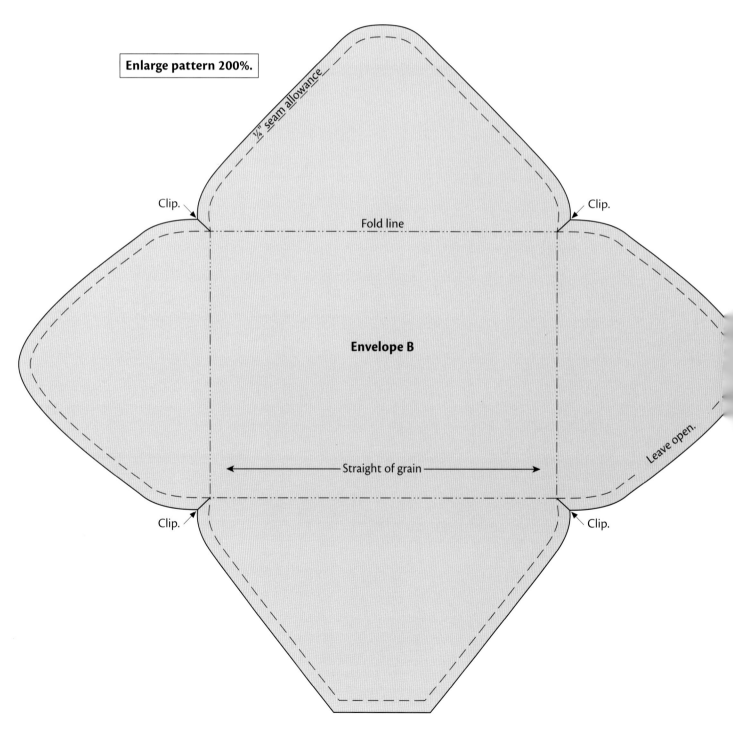

Enlarge pattern 200%.

¼" seam allowance

Clip.   Fold line   Clip.

Envelope B

Straight of grain

Leave open.

Clip.   Clip.

Enlarge pattern 200%.

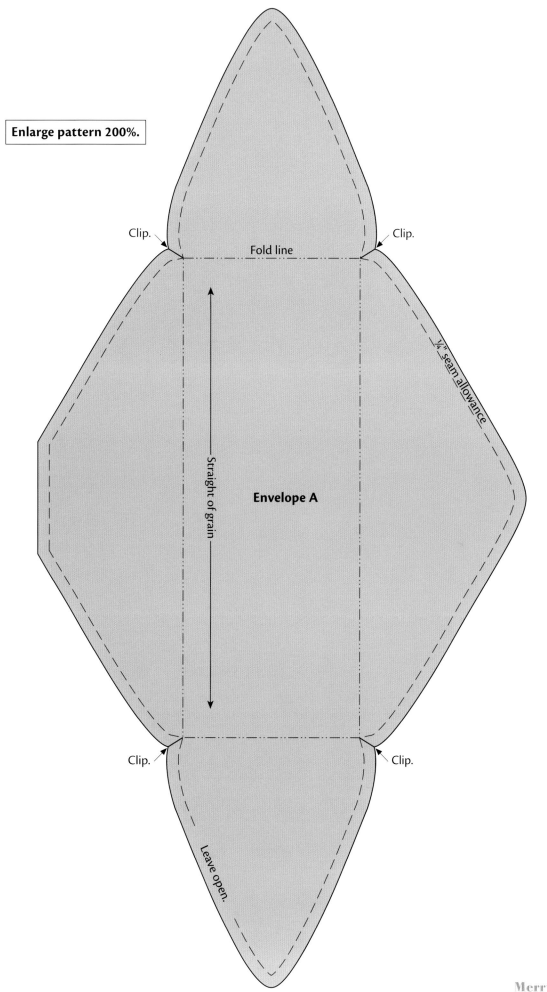

Clip.

Clip.

Fold line

¼" seam allowance

Straight of grain

Envelope A

Clip.

Clip.

Leave open.

Peppermint Dish

Skill Level: Confident Beginner ❄❄

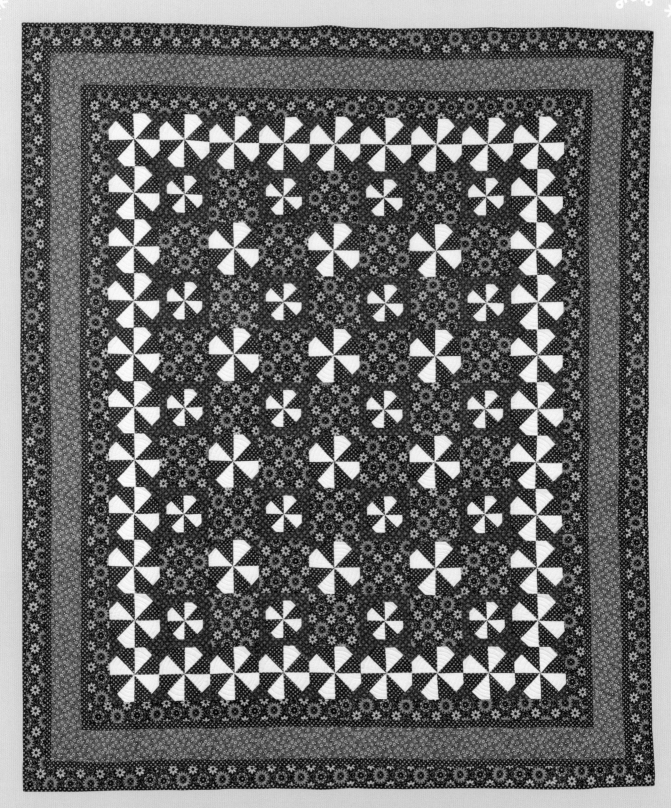

Finished Quilt: 62½" x 72½" ✳ **Finished Block:** 5" x 5"

WRAP IT UP! Too much candy at Christmas? Never happens—just ask any little boy or girl! As for grownups, we appreciate candy that we can enjoy without any calories, so have as many peppermints as you want with this quilt. To make your candy dish as pretty as you can, pick a fanciful print for the background.

Of course, this looks like Christmas candy, but think beyond red-and-white peppermints. Can you picture brightly colored beach balls over a background of fish? — *Susan*

MATERIALS

Yardage is based on 42"-wide fabric.

$2\frac{1}{3}$ yards of red print for peppermints, accent borders, and binding

2 yards of print for alternate blocks and for the innermost and outermost borders

$1\frac{1}{2}$ yards of dark green print for blocks

$1\frac{1}{4}$ yards of white-on-white print for peppermints

$\frac{7}{8}$ yard of medium green print for middle border

$3\frac{7}{8}$ yards of fabric for backing

68" x 78" piece of batting

CUTTING

All measurements include $\frac{1}{4}$"-wide seam allowances.

From the red print, cut:

9 strips, $3\frac{3}{8}$" x 42"; crosscut into 96 squares, $3\frac{3}{8}$" x $3\frac{3}{8}$"

3 strips, $2\frac{5}{8}$" x 42"; crosscut into 40 squares, $2\frac{5}{8}$" x $2\frac{5}{8}$"

13 strips, $1\frac{1}{4}$" x 42"

7 strips, $2\frac{3}{4}$" x 42"

From the white-on-white print, cut:

9 strips, $3\frac{3}{8}$" x 42"; crosscut into 96 squares, $3\frac{3}{8}$" x $3\frac{3}{8}$"

3 strips, $2\frac{5}{8}$" x 42"; crosscut into 40 squares, $2\frac{5}{8}$" x $2\frac{5}{8}$"

From the dark green print, cut:

10 strips, 2" x 42"; crosscut into 192 squares, 2" x 2"

3 strips, $1\frac{1}{2}$" x 42"; crosscut into 80 squares, $1\frac{1}{2}$" x $1\frac{1}{2}$"

2 strips, 4" x 42"; crosscut into 40 rectangles, $1\frac{1}{4}$" x 4"

2 strips, $5\frac{1}{2}$" x 42"; crosscut into 40 rectangles, $1\frac{1}{4}$" x $5\frac{1}{2}$"

From the print for alternate blocks and borders, cut:

5 strips, $5\frac{1}{2}$" x 42"; crosscut into 31 squares, $5\frac{1}{2}$" x $5\frac{1}{2}$"

14 strips, $2\frac{1}{2}$" x 42"

From the medium green print, cut:

7 strips, $3\frac{1}{2}$" x 42"

MAKING THE BLOCKS

1. Using a soft-lead pencil and a see-through ruler, draw a diagonal line from corner to corner on the wrong side of each white 3⅜" and 2⅝" square and on each dark green 2" and 1½" square.

2. With right sides together, pair a red 3⅜" square with a white 3⅜" square. Stitch ¼" from *each side* of the drawn line. Cut on the drawn line. Open each unit and press the seam allowance toward the red. Trim the extended corners. Using all the red and white 3⅜" squares will yield 192 triangle squares.

Make 192.

3. Sew all the triangle squares together in pairs as shown and press toward the red.

Make 96.

4. Sew all the units from step 3 together in pairs to make pinwheels as shown. Before pressing, remove the vertical stitches in the seam allowance on both sides of the pinwheel unit. Then press the seam allowances in opposite directions. Pressing the seam allowances in opposite directions reduces the bulk at this intersection and creates a tiny pinwheel on the wrong side.

Remove stitches in vertical seams.

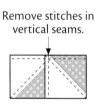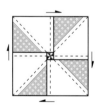

Make 48.

5. Place a dark green 2" square at each corner of a pinwheel as shown. Stitch on the drawn lines. Trim the seams to ¼" and press the triangles toward the corners. Repeat on all 48 pinwheels. Set these blocks aside for now.

Make 48.

6. Using the red 2⅝" squares, the white 2⅝" squares, and the dark green 1½" squares, repeat steps 2–5 to make 20 smaller pinwheels.

7. Add a dark green 1¼" x 4" rectangle to each side of a small pinwheel and press the seams toward the dark green. Add a 1¼" x 5½" rectangle to the top and bottom of the block and press. Repeat to make 20 blocks.

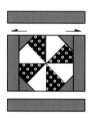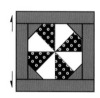

Make 20.

ASSEMBLING THE QUILT TOP

1. For the top and bottom rows, sew nine large Pinwheel blocks together. Press in one direction.

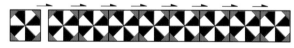

Make 2.

2. Arrange two large Pinwheel blocks, four small Pinwheel blocks, and three 5½" alternate blocks as shown. Sew the blocks together. Press in one direction. Make five rows.

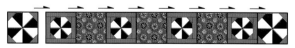

Make 5.

3. Arrange five large Pinwheel blocks and four 5½" alternate blocks as shown. Sew the blocks together and press in one direction. Make four rows.

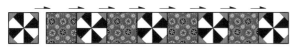

Make 4.

4. Referring to the layout diagram, arrange the rows in the proper order, alternating the direction of the seam allowances from row to row so that the seams oppose each other. Join the rows and press.

5. Measure through the vertical quilt center. Using the 2½" border-fabric strips, cut two pieces to this measurement, joining the strips as necessary. Sew the strips to the sides of the quilt and press the seam allowances toward the outside of the quilt.

6. Measure through the horizontal quilt center. Using the 2½" border-fabric strips, cut two pieces to this measurement, joining the strips as necessary. Sew these to the top and bottom of the quilt and press the seam allowances toward the outside.

7. Repeat steps 5 and 6 to add the next four borders, using the following strips and pressing all seam allowances to the outside.
   - Second (accent) border: red 1¼"-wide strips
   - Third (middle) border: medium green 3½"-wide strips
   - Fourth (accent) border: red 1¼"-wide strips
   - Fifth (outermost) border: 2½"-wide border-fabric strips

FINISHING YOUR QUILT

1. Layer the quilt top, batting, and backing; then baste, unless you plan to take your quilt to a long-arm machine quilter.

2. Hand or machine quilt as desired.

3. Use the red 2¾" strips to bind the edges.

4. Sew a hanging sleeve to the back of the quilt if desired.

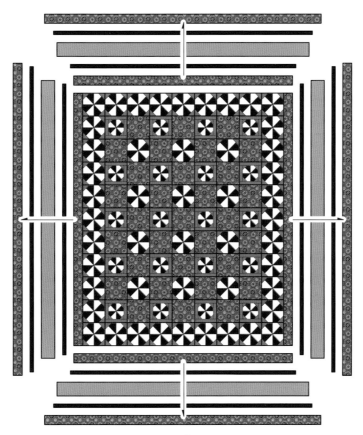

Layout diagram

Christmas Basket

Skill Level: Intermediate ❄ ❄ ❄

Finished Quilt: 37¾" x 37¾"
Finished Basket Block: 18⅞" x 18⅞"

WRAP IT UP! When the winter holidays are over, what fun it would be to welcome spring by making this quilt again, as a "May Basket" filled with flowers of various pastel prints.
— *Loraine*

MATERIALS

Yardage is based on 42"-wide fabric.

1⅓ yards of white print for Basket block, corner triangles, and outer border

⅞ yard of plaid for the Basket block

¾ yard of small-scale holly print for the border of the Basket block, the inner quilt border, and the binding

⅝ yard of large-scale holly print for the Basket block and prairie points

1 yard of dark red print for the poinsettias

1 yard of light red print for the poinsettias

1 yard of green print for the poinsettia leaves

1⅓ yards of fabric for the backing if the fabric is 45" wide (if narrower, you'll need 2⅔ yards)

24" x 36" piece of cotton batting for the poinsettias

43" x 43" piece of batting

4 red buttons, 1¼" diameter

90 yellow star buttons, ⅜" diameter

Thin but sturdy string for making handle bias tube

Optional: 36 heat-set crystals

CUTTING

All measurements include ¼"-wide seam allowances.

From the plaid, cut:

1 strip, 3½" x 42"; crosscut into 9 squares, 3½" x 3½". Cut once diagonally to yield 18 triangles. You will have one unused triangle.

1 bias strip, 2" x 25", for the basket handle

From the large-scale holly print, cut:

1 strip, 3½" x 42"; crosscut into 8 squares, 3½" x 3½". Cut once diagonally to yield 16 half-square triangles. You will have one unused triangle.

4 strips, 3" x 42"; crosscut into 40 squares, 3" x 3"

From the white print, cut:

2 squares, 3½" x 3½"; cut once diagonally to yield 4 triangles

2 strips, 3⅛" x 42"; crosscut into:
    2 pieces, 3⅛" x 11"
    1 piece, 3⅛" x 16¼"
    1 piece, 3⅛" x 18⅞"

1 square, 6⅛" x 6⅛"; cut once diagonally to yield 2 triangles

1 square, 11⅜" x 11⅜"; cut once diagonally to yield 2 triangles

2 squares, 16" x 16", cut once diagonally to yield 4 triangles

4 strips, 3" x 42"; crosscut into:
    4 strips, 3" x 30¾"
    4 squares, 3" x 3"

From the small-scale holly print, cut:

3 strips, 2" x 42"; crosscut into:
    2 strips, 2" x 18⅞"
    2 strips, 2" x 21⅞"

4 strips, 1¼" x 42"; crosscut into:
    2 strips, 1¼" x 30¾"
    2 strips, 1¼" x 37¼"
    4 rectangles, 1¼" x 3"

4 strips, 2¾" x 42"

From the dark red print, cut:

6 squares, 9" x 9"

12 squares, 6½" x 6½"

From the light red print, cut:

6 squares, 9" x 9"

12 squares, 6½" x 6½"

From the green print, cut:

6 squares, 9" x 9"

12 squares, 6½" x 6½"

MAKING THE BASKET BLOCK

1. Sew 15 plaid and 15 large-scale holly print triangles together along the long edges to make triangle squares. Press toward the plaid triangles.

2. Assemble the pieced background as follows, referring to the diagram below and being careful to *orient the triangles as shown*. Letters in the diagram correspond to the assembly sequence.

   a. Sew a plaid triangle to the two 3⅛" x 11" white pieces.

   b. Sew 5 triangle squares together as shown.

   c. Sew 1 white 3½" triangle and 4 triangle squares together as shown.

   d. Sew 1 white 3½" triangle and 3 triangle squares together.

   e. Sew 1 white 3½" triangle and 2 triangle squares together.

   f. Sew 1 white 3½" triangle and 1 triangle square together.

   g. Sew the rows made in steps b–f together as shown.

   h. Sew a triangle cut from the 6⅛" square to the bottom of the basket. (You will have one unused triangle.)

   i. Sew a triangle cut from the 11⅜" square to the top of the basket. (You will have one unused triangle.)

   j. Sew the 3⅛" x 16¼" white piece to the Basket block.

   k. Add the 3⅛" x 18⅞" piece to complete the Basket block.

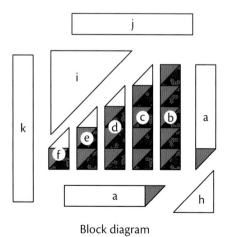

Block diagram

3. To make the basket handle, begin by cutting a 26" length of thin but sturdy string. Fold the 2" x 25" plaid bias strip in half lengthwise, right sides together to make a tube. Place the string inside of the tube, positioning one end of the string at the center along one end of the tube. Sew a ¼" seam across the end of the tube, catching the end of the string securely, and continue to sew down the long edge, being careful not to catch the string in the stitching. Trim the seam allowance to ⅛", and then carefully pull the end of the string to turn the tube right side out. Trim the stitched end from the tube and press the tube flat.

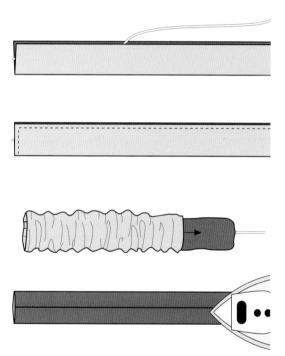

4. At the junction between the basket and handle, carefully open just enough of the seam between the plaid and white triangles to tuck in the ends of the handle. Baste the handle in place. When quilting the quilt, I ran a decorative machine feather stitch along the edge of the handle and basket, eliminating the need for appliquéing the handle in place. If you do not plan on doing this,

stitch the opening closed and attach the handle to the top with hand or machine appliqué.

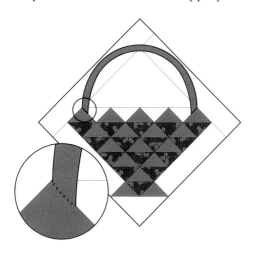

5. Sew 2" x 18⅞" small-scale holly strips to two sides of the Basket block.

6. Sew 2" x 21⅞" small-scale holly strips to the remaining sides of the Basket block.

7. To complete the quilt center, add the triangles cut from the two 16" white squares.

8. Carefully fold and press the forty 3" large-scale holly squares as shown to make prairie points.

Make 40.

9. Arrange and baste the prairie points along the outer edges of the corner triangles as shown, leaving a 1" space at each triangle corner.

10. Sew a 1¼" x 30¾" small-scale holly strip to each side of the quilt center.

11. Sew a white 3" x 30¾" strip to each side of the quilt center.

12. Sew a 1¼" x 37¼" small-scale holly strip to the top and bottom of the quilt.

13. Sew two 3" white squares, two 1¼" x 3" small-scale holly rectangles, and one 3" x 30¾" white strip together as shown. Make two of these units.

14. Sew the units to the top and bottom of the quilt.

Layout diagram

FINISHING YOUR QUILT

1. Layer the quilt top, batting, and backing; then baste, unless you plan to take your quilt to a long-arm quilter.

2. Hand or machine quilt as desired. I quilted a machine feather stitch around the edges of the basket. Remove basting stitches from the handle.

3. Use the 2¾" small-scale holly strips to bind the edges.

4. Add a hanging sleeve if desired.

POINSETTIA FLOWERS

1. To make templates, enlarge patterns A and B on page 19 125% and cut out the shapes. Cut the batting into three 9" squares for the A flowers and six 6½" squares for the B flowers.

2. Place two dark red 9" squares, right sides together, on a 9" square piece of batting. (Pin an A template to this fabric-and-batting sandwich and cut through all of the layers. Remove the template and pin the pieces so the layers will stay together once they've been cut. From *each* of the dark red, light red, and green print 9" squares, cut three poinsettia sandwiches using pattern A. Cut six poinsettia sandwiches from each of the dark red, light red, and green print 6½" squares using pattern B.

3. With the batting side down, sew around each poinsettia using a ¼" seam allowance. Clip the seam allowances and trim the points as shown. Cut a 1"-long slit through the middle of the top layer of fabric. Turn the pieces to the right side and press.

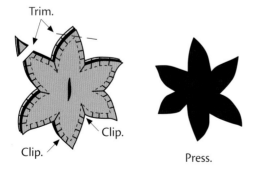

Trim.

Clip.

Clip.

Press.

4. Stitch along the lines indicated on the poinsettia patterns.

5. Stack the poinsettias, with green on the bottom and light red or dark red on top, arranging them so the points are offset.

6. Arrange the poinsettias on the quilt as shown in the photo on page 14. Secure them by tacking through all layers at the poinsettia centers.

7. Attach 10 yellow star buttons to the centers of each poinsettia and embellish with four or five crystals between the buttons if desired Sew the red 1¼" buttons to the corner squares.

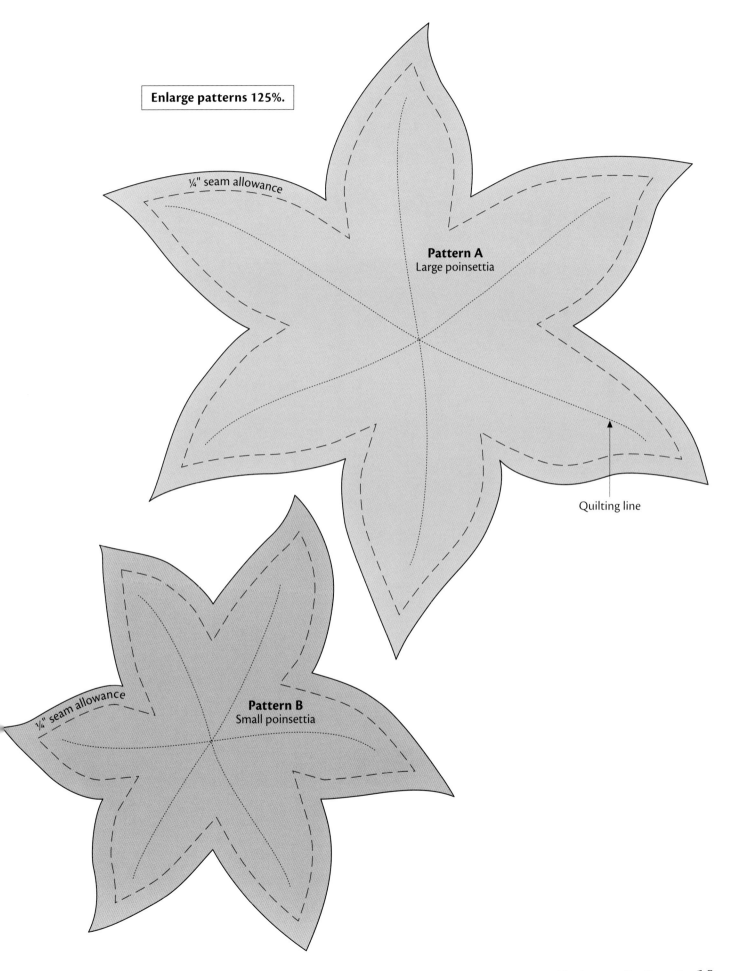

Enlarge patterns 125%.

¼" seam allowance

Pattern A
Large poinsettia

Quilting line

¼" seam allowance

Pattern B
Small poinsettia

Starlight Table Topper
(with Tree Skirt Variation)

Skill Level: Beginner ❄

Finished Quilt: 38½" x 38½" ❄ **Finished Block:** 8" x 8"

WRAP IT UP! Top your holiday table with this Starlight quilt for some extra decorating flair. Add a dazzling centerpiece and flickering candles, and you have a great gathering spot in which to share warm cider and cookies with family and friends. With a little adaptation, this festive table topper can be transformed into a tree skirt. You'll see notes throughout the project on how to make a tree-skirt version.

I originally made this pattern for my daughter's summer wedding. Instead of a ring of stars, I used white and yellow fabrics to make a ring of daisies. And instead of a wreath in the center, I made a checkerboard. Fabric choices can change just about any holiday project into something that can be used year-round. — *Susan*

MATERIALS

Yardage is based on 42"-wide fabric.
1⅜ yards of red print for background
⅝ yard of gold print for star points
⅓ yard of dark green print for wreath
⅓ yard of light green print for wreath
⅓ yard of light gold tone-on-tone print for star centers
⅜ yard of dark green fabric for table-topper binding (if making a tree skirt, you'll need ⅝ yard)
1¼ yards for backing
44" x 44" piece of batting

CUTTING

All measurements include ¼"-wide seam allowances.

From the gold print, cut:

7 strips, 2½" x 42"; crosscut into 108 squares, 2½" x 2½"

From the light gold tone-on-tone print, cut:

1 strip, 4½" x 42"; crosscut into 9 squares, 4½" x 4½"

From the dark green print, cut:

1 strip, 2⅞" x 42"; crosscut into 4 squares, 2⅞" x 2⅞"; cut once diagonally to yield 8 triangles
2 strips, 2½" x 42"

From the red print, cut:

1 strip, 15½" x 42"; crosscut into:
  1 square, 15½" x 15½"; cut twice diagonally to yield 4 triangles
  2 squares, 4⅞" x 4⅞"; cut once diagonally to yield 4 triangles
  1 square, 10½" x 10½", if making the tree skirt
8 strips, 2½" x 42"; crosscut into:
  36 squares, 2½" x 2½"
  36 pieces, 2½" x 4½"
  4 pieces, 2½" x 8½"
5 strips, 1½" x 42"; crosscut into:
  For table topper: 2 pieces 1½" x 8½"
  For table topper: 2 pieces, 1½" x 10½"
  For either table topper or tree skirt: 8 pieces, 1½" x 18½"

From the light green print, cut:

1 strip, 2½" x 42"; crosscut into 4 squares, 2½" x 2½"
2 strips, 2½" x 42"

From the dark green binding fabric, cut:

For table topper: 4 strips, 2¾" x 42"
For tree skirt: 2¾"-wide bias strips to total 210"

MAKING THE BLOCKS

1. Using a soft lead pencil and a see-through ruler, draw a line from corner to corner on the back of each gold 2½" square.

2. With right sides together, position gold 2½" squares on opposite corners of a light gold tone-on-tone 4½" square as shown. Stitch on the drawn lines. Trim ¼" from the stitching lines and press the triangles and seam allowances toward the corner. Repeat on the remaining corners.

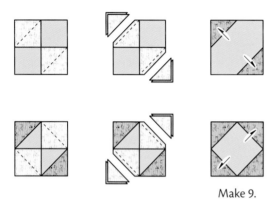

Make 9.

3. With right sides together, position a gold 2½" square on a red 2½" x 4½" piece as shown. Stitch, trim, and press. Repeat for the other end of the piece.

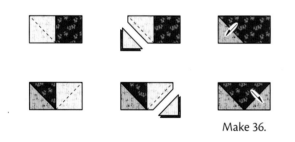

Make 36.

4. Arrange the Ohio Star block as shown, using the units from steps 2 and 3 and red 2½" squares. Sew each row, pressing as shown. Then join the rows.

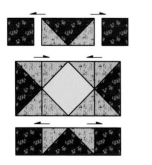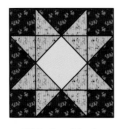

Ohio Star block.
Make 9.

MAKING THE WREATH

1. For the wreath corner blocks, sew a dark green triangle to a light green 2½" square as shown and press toward the triangle. Add another dark green triangle and press again.

Make 4.

2. Join the unit to a small red triangle and press toward the red.

Wreath corner.
Make 4.

3. Join a light green 2½" strip to a dark green 2½" strip as shown. Press toward the dark green. Make 2 strip sets. Cut twenty 2½"-wide segments from the strip sets.

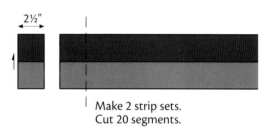

2½"

Make 2 strip sets.
Cut 20 segments.

4. Sew five segments from step 3 together as shown to make one side of the wreath. Make 4.

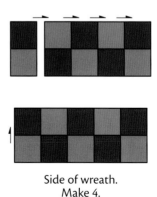

Side of wreath.
Make 4.

ASSEMBLING THE QUILT TOP

1. *If you are making the table topper,* sew red 1½" x 8½" strips to the sides of one Ohio Star block. Then add 1½" x 10½" strips to the top and bottom as shown. This is the center unit. *If you are making the tree skirt,* the center unit will be the red 10½" square, and you'll have one extra Ohio Star block for another project.

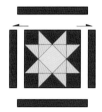

Make 1
for table topper.

2. For both the table topper and the tree skirt, sew a red 2½" x 8½" piece between two Ohio Star blocks. Press toward the center strip. Add red 1½" x 18½" strips to the top and bottom of the section. Press toward the red strips.

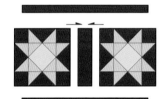 

Make 4.

3. Arrange the wreath center as shown. Sew the sections into rows. Then join the rows and press.

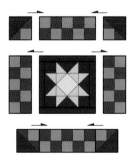 

Table topper wreath center

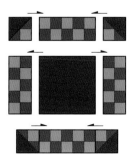 

Tree skirt wreath center

4. Arrange the large red triangles, star sections, and wreath center as shown. Sew into rows. Join the rows and press.

Table topper

Tree skirt

FINISHING YOUR QUILT

1. Layer the quilt top, batting, and backing; then baste, unless you plan to take your quilt to a long-arm machine quilter.

2. Hand or machine quilt as desired.

3. *If you are making the table topper,* skip this step and proceed to step 4. *For the tree skirt,* draw a 6"-diameter circle in the center of the quilt and mark a straight line from the circle to the outside of the quilt as shown. Cut along the line and cut out the circle.

 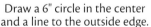 

Draw a 6" circle in the center
and a line to the outside edge.

Cut on drawn lines.

4. *For the table topper,* use the dark green 2¾" x 42" strips to bind the edges. *For the tree skirt,* use the 2¾"-wide bias strips to finish the edges.

Candy Sticks

Skill Level: Intermediate ❄❄❄

Finished Quilt: 55" x 76"

Finished Block A: 2" x 21" ✳ **Finished Block B:** 2" x 10"

WRAP IT UP! For a playful change of season, sew this collection of candy sticks in prints of red, white, and blue to create a dazzling patriotic quilt fit for a summer picnic! — *Loraine*

MATERIALS

Yardage is based on 42"-wide fabric unless otherwise specified.

3⅝ yards of white print for the candy-stick A and B blocks

2½ yards of green dot print for the outer border, inner border, and sashing

1⅞ yards of white foundation fabric for stabilzing the candy-stick blocks*

1⅓ yards of red print for the middle border and the binding

¼ yard *or* 1 fat quarter *each* of 38 different bright prints for the blocks

4 yards of fabric for backing

82" x 61" piece of batting

*If your fabric does not have at least 43" of usable width, you will need 3 yards.

CUTTING

All measurements include ¼"-wide seam allowances.

From the white print, cut:

57 strips, 2" x 42"; crosscut into 114 strips, 2" x 18"

From *each* of the 38 different prints, cut:

2 strips, 2" x 42", crosscut into 3 strips, 2" x 18" (228 total)

From the foundation fabric, cut:*

24 strips, 2½" x 43"; crosscut 19 of the strips into 38 pieces, 2½" x 21½". Crosscut 5 of the strips into 14 pieces, 2½" x 10½".

*If your usable fabric is narrower than 43", you will need to cut thirty-eight 2½" x 42" strips. From 14 strips, cut one 2½" x 10½" piece and one 2½" x 21½" piece each. Cut the remainder of the strips into 24 pieces, 2½" x 21½".

From the *crosswise* grain of the green dot print, cut:

3 strips, 1½" x 42"; crosscut into 37 rectangles, 1½" x 2½"

From the *lengthwise* grain of the green dot print, cut:

14 strips, 1½" x 65½"
2 strips, 2½" x 68"
2 strips, 2½" x 51"
2 strips, 1½" x 76"
2 strips, 1½" x 57"

From the red print, cut:

7 strips, 3½" x 42"
7 strips, 2¾" x 42"

MAKING THE BLOCKS

1. Sew together three white print and three bright strips, alternating the white and bright prints and offsetting each strip by 1½" as shown. Press toward the darker fabric.

2. Align the 45°-angle line of your ruler with a seam line and cut three 2½"-wide segments as shown.

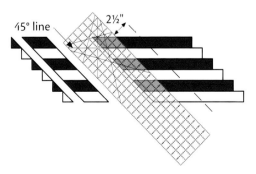

Cut 3 strips at a 45° angle.

3. Join two of the segments as shown. Press toward the darker fabric.

4. Trim the section to measure 2½" x 21½".

5. Place the pieced strip on top of a 2½" x 21½" foundation piece, and machine baste down the center. Basting stabilizes the pieced unit and prevents it from stretching as it's added to the quilt.

Block A.
Make 38.

6. Repeat steps 1–5 to make a total of 38 A blocks, being careful to trim each block so that the stripes are identically placed. In the photo on page 24, you can see that the stripes at the bottom of the longer A blocks are all trimmed so a tiny white triangle is showing.

7. To make block B, trim the third segment cut in step 2 to measure 2½" x 10½" as shown. Place the pieced unit on top of a 2½" x 10½" foundation piece and machine baste down the center. Make fourteen 2½" x 10½" B blocks, being careful to cut each block so that the stripes are identically placed.

Block B.
Make 14.

ASSEMBLING THE QUILT TOP

1. Join two green dot 1½" x 2½" sashing rectangles and three A blocks as shown. Press toward the sashing. Make a total of 8 rows.

Make 8.

2. Sew three green dot 1½" x 2½" sashing rectangles, two A blocks, and two B blocks as shown. Press toward the sashing. Make a total of 7 rows.

Make 7.

3. Join 15 rows and 14 green dot 1½" x 65½" sashing pieces, alternating the block rows as shown. Press toward the sashing.

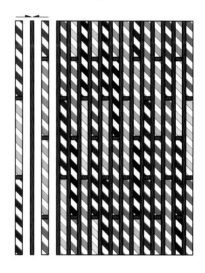

4. Remove the basting stitches from the blocks.

ADDING THE BORDERS

1. Measure the quilt through the vertical center. Cut two border pieces to this measurement from the 2½" x 68" green dot strips. Sew the borders to the sides, referring to the photo on page 24 if needed. Press toward the border.

2. Measure the quilt through the horizontal center. Cut two border pieces to this measurement from the 2½" x 51" green dot strips. Sew these to the top and bottom of the quilt. Press toward the borders.

3. To add the red middle border, repeat steps 1 and 2 using the red print 3½" x 42" strips, joining the strips as necessary.

4. To add the green dot outer border, repeat steps 1 and 2 using the 1½" x 76" and 1½" x 57" strips.

FINISHING YOUR QUILT

1. Layer quilt top, batting, and backing; then baste.

2. Hand or machine quilt as desired.

3. Use the red 2¾" strips to bind the edges.

Hand Warmers

Skill Level: Confident Beginner ❄❄

Finished Quilt: 57½" x 69½" ✳ **Finished Block:** 9" x 9"

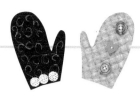

WRAP IT UP! Perfect winter weather calls for mittens to keep fingers warm while you're making snowballs and romping in the snow. Once inside the house again, curl up by the fireplace with some hot cocoa and this quilt to warm up those fingers—and toes and nose. More than a holiday quilt, this design will carry you through the late fall, into the New Year, and beyond.

The key to this quilt is the scrappy use of a variety of black and white prints contrasted with bright fabrics for the mittens. So check your fat-quarter stash, and then add some new ones to the mix. Pore over your button jars for an array of colors and dimensions. I gathered many of these buttons on a trip to Europe and thought this was a great way to showcase my souvenirs. — *Susan*

MATERIALS

Yardage is based on 42"-wide fabric unless otherwise specified.

14 fat quarters of assorted black prints for blocks and sashing

8 fat quarters of assorted white prints for sashing and outer border

1 yard *total* of assorted bright print scraps for mitten appliqués

⅝ yard of black print for binding

3½ yards of fabric for backing

63" x 75" piece of batting

Template plastic

⅝ yard of fine tulle for the appliqués (optional)

Monofilament for invisible machine appliqué (optional)

120 bright buttons, ½" to ⅞" diameter

96 white buttons, ⅝" diameter

CUTTING

All measurements include ¼"-wide seam allowances.

From *each* fat quarter of assorted black prints, cut:
5 strips, 3½" x 21" (70 total)

From *each* fat quarter of assorted white prints, cut:
3 strips, 2" x 21"; crosscut into 25 squares, 2" x 2" (200 total)
3 strips, 3½" x 21"; crosscut into 14 squares, 3½" x 3½" (112 total)

From the black print for binding, cut:
7 strips, 2¾" x 42"

MAKING THE BLOCKS AND SASHING

1. Arrange the 3½"-wide black strips into 22 sets of 3 strips, varying the prints from group to group. You'll have 4 strips left over for another project, but this gives you enough variety to arrange all your sets. Sew each set of 3 strips into a strip set as shown. Press 11 strips sets so that the seam allowances go toward the center, and press the other 11 strip sets so that the seam allowances go toward the outside.

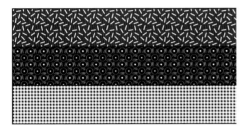

Make 22 strip sets.

2. Cut five 3½" segments from each strip set as shown. You'll have 110 segments, but you'll use only 109.

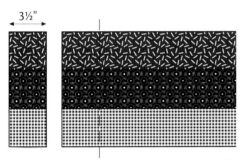

Cut 5 segments from each strip set (110 total).

PIECING THE SASHING

1. Using a soft-lead pencil and a see-through ruler, draw a diagonal line from corner to corner on the wrong side of each white 2" square.

2. With right sides together, place the squares on opposite corners of a black segment in which the seam allowances are pressed toward the center, as shown. Stitch on the diagonal lines. Trim ¼" from the stitching lines and press the triangles and their seam allowances toward the corners. Place squares on the remaining corners. Stitch, trim, and press as before. You will have four unused white 2" squares. Be sure that all the black seam allowances are pressed toward the center. When the quilt has been assembled, all the seam allowances will nest nicely. Make 49 sashing sections.

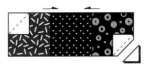 

Make 49 sections.

Making the Mitten Blocks

1. For each Nine Patch block, sew three black segments together, nesting the seam allowances as shown. You may need to re-press some segments so that the seam allowances match the diagram, but if you press as shown, all your seam allowances will nest when you add the sashing, and your quilt will lie neatly flat.

 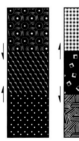  

Make 20.

2. Using the pattern on page 31 and your preferred appliqué method, cut and appliqué 20 pairs of mittens to the Nine Patch blocks. Whatever appliqué method you choose, be sure to position the mittens at least ½" from the edges of the block. The "Invisible Machine Appliqué" instructions that follow outline how I appliquéd my mittens.

Make 20.

INVISIBLE MACHINE APPLIQUÉ

Especially if you don't have a lot of appliqué experience, this method is an easy way to achieve a turned edge for the appliqués. It also allows you to use an invisible stitch without all the handwork.

1. Trace the appliqué pattern on page 31 onto template plastic and cut out your template.

2. Trace the template onto the wrong side of a bright print and then cut out the mitten shape on the drawn line. Cut one regular and one reversed mitten from each fabric so that you have 20 matching pairs.

3. Cut the fine tulle into 20 rectangles, 4¼" x 5¾". Center a mitten, right side down, over the tulle. Pin the layers together, and using a straight stitch, carefully stitch all the way around the mitten using a scant ¼" seam. Between the mitten and the thumb, clip the "V" in the seam allowance.

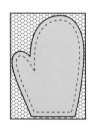

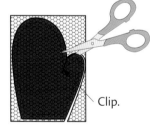

Clip.

4. In the middle of the mitten, cut a slash only through the tulle layer so that you can turn the appliqué shape right side out. From the cotton side, gently press the edges so that the seam allowances lie neatly flat. The tulle is the trick to turning and holding the appliqué edges in this method!

5. Attach an open-toe appliqué foot to your machine. Thread it with monofilament in the top, and in the bobbin, use cotton thread that matches your background. Set your machine to the blind hem stitch, with the stitch size set about 1 mm long and 1 mm wide. You may need to adjust the stitch length and width until you find what works the best for you. Do some practicing before stitching your project.

6. Place a pair of mittens on a Nine Patch block, right sides up, and at least ½" from the edges of the block. Position an appliqué under the presser foot. You want the right swing of your stitch to pierce the background next to the appliqué and the left swing to catch the appliqué. Stitch around the mitten, overlapping the starting point by a few stitches to secure.

Left swing position

Right swing position

7. To reduce bulk, cut away the background fabric behind the appliqué. Use small, sharp scissors and work from the back of the block. Trim away only the background layer, leaving a seam allowance about ¼"-wide inside the stitching line.

ASSEMBLING THE QUILT TOP

1. For each sashing row, arrange four pieced sashing sections between five white 3½" squares as shown. Sew the pieces together and press toward the white squares.

Make 6 sashing rows.

2. For each mitten row, arrange four Mitten blocks between five sashing sections as shown. Sew the rows together and press toward the Mitten blocks.

Make 5 block rows.

3. Arrange the mitten rows between the sashing rows. Join the rows and press toward the mitten rows.

4. For each side border, join 21 white 3½" squares and press the seam allowances so that they will nest with the quilt-center seam allowances. Add the side borders to the center. For the top and bottom borders, join 19 white 3½" squares for each border. Again, press the seam allowances so that they will nest with the seam allowances in the quilt center. Sew the borders to the top and bottom of the quilt center.

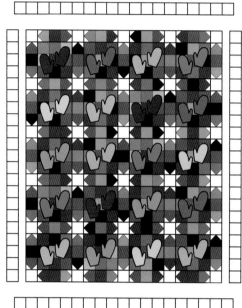

Layout diagram

FINISHING YOUR QUILT

1. Layer the quilt top, batting, and backing; then baste, unless you plan to take your quilt to a long-arm machine quilter.

2. Hand or machine quilt as desired.

3. Use the black 2¾" strips to bind the edges.

4. Embellish the mittens with your collection of bright buttons. Place them as shown in the photo on page 27 or create your own scheme. Then add the white buttons to embellish the snowflakes.

5. Sew a hanging sleeve to the back of the quilt if desired.

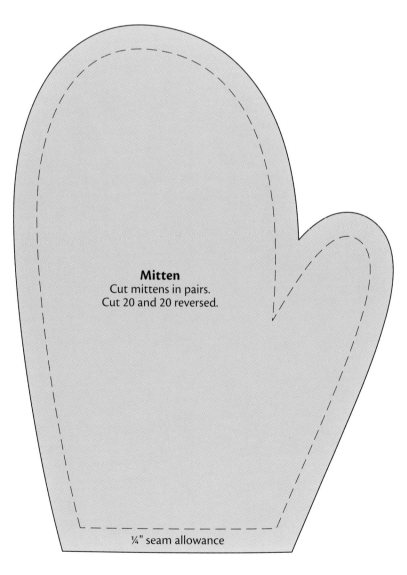

Mitten
Cut mittens in pairs.
Cut 20 and 20 reversed.

¼" seam allowance

About the Authors

Loraine Manwaring

Susan Nelsen

Loraine Manwaring started sewing at the age of eight when she received a small Singer sewing machine as a gift. When her children were young, she began teaching basic sewing to a women's group at church, and this led to teaching beginning quilting classes. She has been teaching various fabric arts ever since and for years has designed her own patterns and quilting projects. She has written one other book, *All Buttoned Up* (Martingale & Company, 2006) with her sister, Susan Nelsen. She holds a degree in elementary education from Utah State University. Loraine and her husband, Mark, raised their family in Washington State and currently live in northern Idaho. They are the parents of five grown children. Loraine enjoys creating quilt designs, traveling the world, and spending time with her grandchildren.

Colors, fabrics, design; mixing and matching; stitching—and sometimes restitching—are all part of the quilting process that Susan loves. She thrives on designing and is the owner of Rasmatazz Designs, a quilt-pattern company and long-arm quilting business. She has published numerous patterns and three other books. Besides designing, she teaches quilting and edits quilting books and projects. She might be found at her computer, her sewing machine, or her long-arm machine at any time, day or night. Susan and her husband, Ken, settled in southern Idaho after his retirement from the United States Air Force. They have three terrific sons and a talented daughter—all married now, and Susan and Ken enjoy the role of grandparents to their grandchildren. Susan can be contacted via her Web site, www.rasmatazzdesigns.com.